SOLAR PERPLEXUS

ALSO BY DEAN YOUNG

SOLAR PERPLEXUS

DEAN YOUNG

COPPER CANYON PRESS

PORT TOWNSEND, WASHINGTON

Cover art: Dean Young

Copper Canyon Press is in residence at Fort Worden State Park in Port Townsend, Washington, under the auspices of Centrum. Centrum is a gathering place for artists and creative thinkers from around the world, students of all ages and backgrounds, and audiences seeking extraordinary cultural enrichment.

LIBRARY OF CONGRESS CATALOGING-IN-PUBLICATION DATA
Names: Young, Dean, 1955– author.
Title: Solar perplexus / Dean Young.
Description: Port Townsend, Washington : Copper Canyon Press, [2019]
Identifiers: LCCN 2019016850 | ISBN 9781556595721 (hardcover : alk. paper)
Classification: LCC PS3575.O782 A6 2019 | DDC 811/.54—dc23
LC record available at https://lccn.loc.gov/2019016850

9 8 7 6 5 4 3 2 FIRST PRINTING

COPPER CANYON PRESS
Post Office Box 271
Port Townsend, Washington 98368

www.coppercanyonpress.org

for James Tate & Tomaž Šalamun

And in the train made of glass turtles
You won't have to pull the emergency cord
You'll arrive alone on that lost shore
Where a star will alight on your luggage of sand

André Breton

To go down in flames
means you're not burning hard enough
flames go up

Li Long Zu

CONTENTS

SOLAR PERPLEXUS

Reality

I don't know what people mean
by reality.
Is it the ocean
which I've always loved
no matter its chitinous claws
or the sky everything falls through
or those scary-ass mites
that live on our eyelids
or the rain of diamonds on Saturn?
Whatever it is,
I'm sure I've tried to avoid it
ever since my teachers and ex-girlfriends
threatened one day it would dawn on me
in a way that made me think
that dawn would just make everything darker.
Now when I think of reality,
I see one of those beige plastic covers
over the hospital's main entry.
We're surrounded by zinnias
trying to sneak up on us
and an indeterminate rumbling fills the air.
Here's my birth certificate,
see if you can make sense of it.

Infinitives

To pick up where Tomaž left off.
To pick off another oniony layer
down to the eye. To chomp.
To walk around all day buttoned wrong.
Light coming from rocks, the little froggy
jumps even though he hasn't been wound up.
Here's where the wolves before us drank.
Too long we have cock-blocked
day from mating with night.
The world is bluer than I thought.
To be stopped at security
for crying.
For something wrapped in foil.
For the soul finding its face.
For liquid.
I don't know if I forget
my dreams or life more.
To smudge out the features.
To endure blasted.
To nestle in a dark place
inside the floodlight.
To contain multiples.
To calm the hurt animal.
To be inside another.
To have been there all along.

Newborn Poem

First off, welcome and beware—humans
don't have coherent nuclei so
you can't predict which way they'll lurch,
which flowers are most magnetic, or if
it's going to rain. Ambulatory but
nonetheless confined like luna moths
running out of air in glass skulls,
something the French Revolution tried to stop,
cutting each other's head off as proof.
As in a love affair. As when a trumpet
hovers in the air. The average cloud
outweighs a bus. That strewn dust above
is the universe. Usually humans lose it
when confronted with angelic apparatus,
cliff drops, star charts, the matchstick
of the scarecrow's heart, any declaration
of love. So don't bother warning anyone
although waving frantically is good cardio
and waking up screaming good for the lungs.

Goals for Recovery

What I wanted most when I finally got out
were pizza, sex, and Sun Ra, not in any order.
The fun part of being a ghost where birds
dive through your chest and you can't be stopped
from strolling bank vaults
wasn't happening yet but at least when I drink
red, it doesn't drain out. It augments.
Like pennies in soil turn hydrangeas blue.
Like Franklin discovering electricity resides
in the sky, inventing a new form of suicide.
Like an ancient Chinese poet so drunk
even the moon in a puddle seems sober.
Like overtipping the 3-fingered girl who cuts
my hair to help get her boyfriend out of jail.
Like swimming farther than anyone ever has
in a shot glass. Like how every rose starts out
and ends up an explosion. Like a child lost in the woods
can't help but walk in circles. Like eye contact
with an ostrich. Like packing the smallest
suitcase, never intending to come back.
Radiant the wolf-face of my flashlight.
Radiant the chamomile of my convalescence.
Once a stranger in a bar insisted he owed me
100 bucks but I only accepted 25. Once
a stranger handed me a bottle of champagne
in a line of backed-up traffic behind
a pileup in a tunnel. Then kissed me. Hard.

At Shangyang's

Friends, it's difficult to talk about poetry
which is why we're all talking at once
about something else: who can use whose
mythology and bathroom, magic mushrooms,
phlogiston, Czechoslovakian milk production,
a single use of the word *black* in Ovid.
Shining discs have been spotted siphoning
off libraries dot by dot. Did we pump
blood back into the construct just
to club ourselves to death with hood ornaments?
News from the crystal world isn't good.
News from the elephant's worse.
But what's pirouetting in the fire
might not be only ash.
One of us brings a fang.
In rushing water, another sees the face of his father.
One lights his cave with chrysanthemums.

Tail Feathers

I arrived by rain.
A few metallic swoops went through.
A cauliflower was also a mirror.
X-rays discovered a pile of skulls
beneath Cézanne's heap of peaches.
Plenty of salt, blood, and cognac.
What I knocked my head against
turned out to be crystal.
A room hummed.
The big kids told the little kids
you'd die if you touched the door.
It felt warm.
It felt soft.
Moist.
Like flames.

What We've Gotten Ourselves Into

D moves his mouse closer to the rocket.
S throws up on the stone lions.
N turns the score upside down
and plays it that way, rubato,
smaller pieces rising on fire
to vanish like metaphors. No
better time than now to read Lorca.
One idea is a door can be opened
by pressing your forehead against
a sheet of paper. I brought my own
black wire and opiates. Another
is to plant a giant, elemental,
too-bitter-to-eat fruit-bearing
question in your mind and stare
at the sea until the sea becomes
your mind, which will feel hyper-
hygienic at first. Go ahead, spend years
in a steel cage counting to 140,
every evening trying to pick the lock
with a duck feather but it's not
a competition. I know a guy who
knew a guy who had some sort of castle connection
but it is silly to expect glaciers
to share. For me, it's the backyard,
maybe a graveyard or sitting in an old
broken rowboat until the silvery
spear of Apollo pierces my left ear
producing some offbeat ectoplasmic squawks
it's my job to translate.
Of course it hurts.

Spontaneous Butterfly

It's hard to get people to dance
in daylight. On campus, the Christians
have put up a board with the question
What happens when you die?
and plenty of room below.
By the time my class follows one poet's
heavenly rebuff and sets up a tribunal
to condemn another, it's covered.
Nothing, you rot. An angel
lifts the soul from the torment
of the body. The electrical activity
of the brain stops. You're still fat.
You see god. You see dog. A coyote
carries your heart over the river
to be weighed. Over the river
and through the woods to grandma's house
we go. You're famous. You're forgotten.
You don't have to pay taxes. Or study
for fucking biochem. Or not get enough.
Only once have I thought a dark horse
was galloping toward me
in a trespassed field at night
and been right. So far.

Medical Myths

If you put your ear against it,
even a door locked in a dream
has a throb. A current.
Daisies sizzle.
A tiny astronaut makes up
the snowman's heart.
Given my travel restrictions,
my flopping levitations,
the trumpet hovering in the séance,
the staples in my sternum
causing the guard's consternation
same as any liquid especially
tequila, especially tears.
Given my present underwater pallor,
the line of zeros conspiring
my bank account and the agatizing
pressures causing translucence
in what it doesn't crush,
someone else is going to have to put
an orange on Paul Éluard's grave.

Archaic Torso of Me Too

There was the guy in the next room
screaming he wanted some goddamn sugar.
There was the lady who my first night
conscious tried to get me to pray while
a falcon-headed shade carried off
my biowaste, hexes welting the walls—
she was also a hallucination. How
I was strapped to the face of a sundial,
names of drugs like archangels,
the breathing machine pulling in
an Army–Navy game and tolling
like Big Ben. Hovering beside me,
another me entirely free of pain
like the idea of a rainbow beside
a fading rainbow. Huff of alcohol,
fentanyl, urine, red beets. The one
I made leave because he couldn't stop
acting triumphant. It wasn't only death
in costume. But always there was my darling
who'd kiss me even though the pulse-spike
would bring nurses running.

Flight Path

Curiosities avail not. The body
is a shoe box, precious tanglement
of kelp, china doll-head fit perfectly
in the palm crushing it or not. Novelists
and volcanologists make crumbs.
Measurements and linguistics
avail not. The space program
makes crumbs. Doesn't barking
open an aperture? Doesn't this wine
taste like stone? Larvae also grow
wings, equipages of crumbs.
Are pain and euphoria not bosom twins?
Doesn't disarray also attend?
Here comes Boris Karloff
to make Frankenstein crumbs.
My heart too is secondhand.
Watch me trying to flag down
help on a deserted, snowy road,
laugh at the protocol while
sitting in an exit row, talk
of Van Gogh in a swishy hotel bar,
estranged peanuts in a glowing
neural bowl, bartender of aluminum
and smoke. Don't we try to find the sea
every night, an ethereal core
in blocks of granite, owls
attacking us? Don't we work hard
at nothing while nothing works harder
on us? Surely a single brush with an ant

is divinity enough. Tentatively
punching ourselves in the face
makes crumbs. Ditto applying black lipstick
at the rest stop. Aren't we supposed
to be lost? Isn't our desolation
atomic? Aren't we herded back
to the stars? Heaven's bread also crumbles.
Sad child at the zoo, how the hooks
of your empathy get stuck in the elephant
swaying foot to foot slowly going
insane. Insane wind chimes. Insane telephone.
It's the crows in last-second slashes
that bring out the flames of the wheat field.

Demonic Possession Is 9/10 of the Law

What's in cryostasis
should stay in cryostasis.

Do not core-sample the frozen alien.

If the landlord tells you
not to hang a mirror in that room,
do not hang a mirror in that room.

Do not jump off a train in the Carpathians
to investigate a castle ruin.

A stake through the heart
is only half of it.

All flowers eat meat.

Put no faith in a sequel.

The ultimate monster is always the self.

Marriage Poem

Yes, I've made some mistakes
but I know now when hydrogen
or a cricket gets into the bedroom
or a tire keeps leaking or a dog
whines or the cork is black or
an aardvark walks into a bar,
you can't swallow shadow
like vodka even though they taste
the same. Like the ashes of ice.
Like the role you play in someone else's
dream. Like laughter in the periphery
of a Kandinsky. Don't pour bleach
on a tick. Some poisons are best
left to pass through, others upchucked.
The wisdom of life is a fish bone.
Many faces have been etched in stone
then blasted away. King of what?
The mind is made of silver dots.
Do not shoot radiation into
the mysterious space-rock. It is an egg.
I am an egg. Thomas Jefferson was an egg.
No wonder his signature flowered
from a feather. My bones are made
of milk. I saw a beautiful baby today
but she wouldn't marry me although
I feel the refusal was unduly influenced
by her matron and some bystanders.
Apparently it's gotten around that
my previous engagement to a tree

ended abruptly with wild recriminations
but I contributed far more than a piggy bank.
Suddenly the blank space in my head
made rhino habitat.
Suddenly my head tuned into Xmas music,
mostly the X. Suddenly my head
had teeth in it. I sat at a table
working a puzzle that was also my head.
We're flowers, not just people.
My head was swallowed by another head
which was also mine, mint-brained,
sulfur-breathed. Here comes a man
made of smoke. It's me. Some people
like to believe the worst, especially those
putting 4 and 4 together to make 3.
Well, one day that baby isn't going to be a baby
and won't be so easily distracted
by random movements or dangling
string. Here's a diamond ring to prove it.
Here's a plankton-toned kiss.
Here's a glove to lift a burning sword,
a house made of twigs.
Here comes the green waterfall.
Here comes the aardvark.
Here comes another man of smoke.
It's still me.

Last Postcard from Šalamun

Half the people in this Tintoretto
don't even know a god is dying
or who is whose figment.
Inside every bird is a message
not necessarily of a better world.
I bet this burning scarecrow
will never walk into a bar again
where everyone doesn't already know the joke.
Every rock moos.
The clock tower's shadow has its face on the ground
and whatever that idiot on the radio's
singing about love, whatever donkey
birthday party, drive-by divorce or
dirty-dancing funeral, all just
bubbles burst like when you're dumb enough
to let flowers fill your chest,
bits of goat head stewing in the aftermath.
One doctor told me not to think
of life as a big breath out
even though I'm already 85% vapor.
Another advised against joining any underground
commotion regardless I'm half-buried myself.
Only twice have I heard talk of blowing up
the moon. Once some engineers intent
on creating a UV shield of lunar dust
and now me as illustration
so please keep me away from Christmas decorations.
The wise man gives nothing away,
keeps the embalming spices for himself.

I wish I had a mule to hug.
A private elevator. A flying rug.
I asked god to set fire to me
and he maketh me molder and stink.
He cracketh spiders over my head
but apparently nothing can rip
this giant withering butterfly off my face.
It's not a circle, it's just bent.
Either I'm suffering from an advanced
hocus-pocus collapse or some splashed-back hex
so now I'm the one waking along in a wet bed
with 50 feet of snake rind on the floor.
When I put on my falling-water suit
I look nothing like falling water.
I try a hard hip-nudge
to loosen the automaton
as when a sheriff wakes a bootlegger,
as when magnolias are put in the lab-rat cages,
as when the fisherman throws the pearl back
in demonstration of an effervescence
that humiliation takes no part
in the imagination and pain
is just glitter in the mind.

Unknown Ode

Historically, the unknown was used
to stanch battlefield wounds.
Now there's a spray. The unknown
assumes too much, says Annabell
trying to break up with herself,
like anyone's here in the first place.
There are rules about touching
someone else's unknown no one's
learning in grade school anymore.
Here's one now.
Boiling point unknown,
cleave disposition, event horizon,
its animal origami unknown
so stop poking.
I thought the idea was not
to have our brains sucked out
by a giant radioactive leech
or an English department
or is that just me? After
the third surgery, I don't scare
so easily but who isn't jumpy
as an astronaut recollecting
crash-landing spontaneously
in the Sea of Tranquility,
O_2 running out?
The news from the moon isn't good.
The news from the glacier's much worse.
Centuries ago, a little girl
could watch a funny bird kicking leaves

until the hand of god came out
and she became Emily Dickinson
and the universe milkweed
as the quantum predicts.
A lot harder now.
It's all paved over.
God's institutionalized. Murderous.
Most of the universe won't show up
and it messes with you
so you envision fish blowing tubas,
yo-yoing angels to flesh things out.
Layer after layer of shellac.
Screws in pianos.
Fingerprints on snowflakes.
First you have to love death
says Éluard, like it's not
his black raincoat saying it,
like anything his raincoat says
isn't stolen from the rain, which
everyone knows around here
hardly ever reaches the ground.

Weird Window Box

You know how strange mystical powers
allow you to move objects with your mind
and talk to dogs
and fly
but when it comes to that nonspecific
colloidal mass you married,
you might as well set yourself on fire in a field
of delphiniums, not that I can wholly recommend
the efficacy of flames without mentioning
it'll probably rain
and there's always something icky left over,
a residue.
How about not being knocked out by a cloud?
Actually, it's not that hard to get blood
from a stone but good luck stopping the bleeding.
Funny how everything can be broken
but how impossible to break free.
All this encryption to go straight to voice mail.
All this metallurgy for a pin.
As far as I know, it's best to leave the knife in.
The rest is paperwork.

Camera Ready

I used to try to watch French movies
out of a nothingness in the head
which was a mark of extreme intelligence
like wearing a black raincoat for pajamas
and watching French movies,
gazing at whatever smoke-filled
woman's ignoring me
through a cloudy raindrop.
Bicycles would just appear, like cats.
Even a balloon could hurt.

Someone Has to Be Lowered into the Whale Skull for the Ambergris

Once I seduced a woman by misquoting
Rilke on the steps of an observatory.
Her mouth tasted like snow.
Have you ever woken upside down?
All of us for a while were birds.
Even a crocodile remembers the egg,
even my dog although her expressive
options are limited to running around
sniffing and barking at I know now
nothing until she turns into a ball
of light. Lilacs pulse, dew
democratizes, wing-nubs ache
the back and by August the grasshoppers
are big as shotgun shells. Under
an oak someone had driven a spike into
the tree had nearly consumed, she broke
up with me then we wandered
through a greenhouse exhibit
of carnivorous orchids and goodbye
hand-fucked in the car so
you can believe me when I say
everything is singing and love
is eternal and wake up and smell the gasoline.

Cyclops Stomp

What makes me happy even though

What makes me happy is this book
of Jim's I bought then walked
to Emily Dickinson's grave
and the little purple parachutist
draped on her fence. I wonder
how often she walked here
with a book of Jim's thinking
the mind is a starfish.
How marvelous to have so many arms.
To be longitudinally blue.
To move neuron-fast.
To resist death.
I miss Amherst
where I never lived.
I miss that triangular café
where a homeless guy told me
about some secret submarine passageway to Russia,
where I was passed a sexually explicit note,
where a huge stuffed bear fell on me
and I was given in recompense
a coupon I never used,
where I saw Zap wonder-struck by a muffin,
where I laughed out loud when David
told me he was in love and laughed louder
when he said who
and they had good noodle soup.
So far, the god with the purple tongue
only had one foot on my chest

which didn't stop me from floating,
didn't stop the whole world from floating.
Light comes from under a locked door.
A dog barks from a tower.
We are all chained to something.
The little burnished bits we're made of
come from exploded stars.
You come from the sky.
I come from Philadelphia.

Dance Event

I'm used to not getting the joke,
maybe even being the joke.
Once a parrot landed on my head
and I dropped a birthday cake
and still have the photographs
of my now ex with that scuba diver.
The thing about a Laundromat at midnight.
The thing about spiders. The best thing
about death is it's a mystery so
you can tell all the experts
to go fuck themselves if that
appeals to you and if it doesn't,
you may already be dead.
Simple test:
Approach a strawberry.
A pulse is kid stuff.
Dance in live ash with feathers
through your earlobes.
Converse with a sapling.
Walk cloud.
Macerate in Cointreau.
Estivate and call home.
Feed a fever fever.
Cradle dawn.
Love everyone.

Flowers in Handcuffs

Not once has Mob Bomb screamed at me
It's all your fault, bouncing
a chrysanthemum off my chest.
Not once has Kangaroo Kush
withheld its affections until
I'm perfectly happy to be dropped off
on a glacier. Blueberry Stardawg
never changed the locks or screwed up
my deductible, not once hurrying me
through the foggy wolf habitat.
It's consensual. A horse-in-the-meadow
kind of thing. Sure, you can shake
a lot of answers out of a drunk monkey
but the monkey won't like it so
maybe the next time you need some answers,
that monkey won't be so cooperative.
Much better to have a head that floats
like a cross between a jellyfish
and an amaryllis bulb. The fox steps
closer. Its envelope is blue.

Early-Bird Matinee

Huge crazy close-up faces, disturbing
situations and themes, long flights
of stairs, cries in the night you never
know what, surgical vistas, a job painting
the T. rex at the miniature golf course
while trying to seduce an already knocked-
up concession girl, gradually increasing
sensitivity to paper cuts, caffeine, voices
in the basement, voices in the hall,
disquisitions on mushroom-picking,
the requisite foaming mouth, shadows
crinkling with something come and gone
or never come at all, explicit howls
like being knee-whacked by a spark plug
falling from outer space like Milton
hitting Blake in the foot, much fumbling
in the coatroom like batshit sexual antics
between inflatable Santas, de rigueur eyeball
ejection because if you're sleeping with
a werewolf, even one made of carpet remnants,
you gotta expect some ganglion on the ceiling
and super-hot, naked devil-dancing Eurotrash
if it's Italian, subliminal messages
tweeted from the big bang, language
especially involving words.
A rocket waits. A mouse lifts a sword.
It's always summer at the lake house
and your parents are away.

Best Man to the Moon

A foot closer seems to come the bride
but she's made of silver dots
same as us. Ours is a wedding to dust.
So fuck dust in the limousine.
Eat all the seedcakes. Fuck
the stuffing out of dust.
Even in a silo, the body isn't safe.
They'll tong it out in chunks.
They have a special bag.
A desiccation process.
Better our dancing cause alarm
among the health-care professionals.
Better lightning smear.
The biggest sandwich in the world.
Every quarter hour a star explodes.
Every 60 seconds fills with jelly.
Friend, lift yourself from
your webby substrate.
Inoculate the daffodils!
Inculcate daffodils!
Do fucking something with daffodils!
It has a pulse, the current
that carries us, laughter too
although not yet close enough
to say about what.

11:45 p.m.

I thought it'd be enough
lily of the valley
cricket drip in pine needles
fog-sip
curlicue of smoke
purple for shadows
morphine for snow
unbroken doll-head found in kelp
not crushing it
not crushing the rose
but I need a door.

Anniversary Poem

When you gave me a walnut,
it was different from when you gave me
a monarch wing which I taped
to my notebook. Other things
I've taped: flattened wildflowers,
a leaf that was in the tub with you,
a few dead ants who were red and black
like Mayan gods. I recommend packing tape,
it's wide and strong and doesn't yellow.
When you gave me the walnut
I wondered if I should eat it,
put it in a drawer with the glove
I found in a rosebush, plant it or give it
to a squirrel to more professionally plant.
We talked it over without talking,
putting our hands inside each other's coat
while snow crystallized small bits
of oblivion which doesn't seem like
people'd have heart attacks shoveling
but you'd be wrong. The walnut
had not come from the millionaire-hippie co-op
where once I ate a rotisserie chicken
in my car in the parking lot for warmth
waiting for a tow-truck jump.
If I had called you, you would
have been in New York which is where
you were. Sometimes I'm there
with you looking at filched treasure
from the pyramids but also in Iowa City,

Berkeley, Bloomington, even Columbia,
Pennsylvania where I was born and learned
to walk down alleys to the river
befriending sad, fenced-in dogs,
not even caring if I ever got married
but if you asked, I would have asked you.

New Restrictions

It doesn't matter how many
Wallace Stevens poems you've memorized
or if you had sex in the graveyard
like an upside-down puppet
or painted your apartment red
so it feels like sleeping inside a heart
or the trees were frozen with ravens
which you sent pictures of to everyone you know
or your pie dough's perfect
or you once ran a sub-5-minute mile
or you're on the last draft
of your mystery novel and still
don't know if the vicar did it
or every morning that summer
you saw a fox stepping through the fog
but it got no closer
or once you helped drag a deer
off the road by the antlers
it blinked
or which song comes from which side
of your mouth as you drive
all night all night all night
or how deep and long you carry
a hitch in your breath after crying
or shot a man in Tennessee
or were so happy in France
or left your favorite scarf in a café,
the one with the birds and terrible art
or the Klimt

or you call your mother once a week
even after she's dead
or can't see a swan without panic
or have almost figured out
what happened to you as a child,
urge, urge, nothing but urge
or 600 daffodils
or a knife in the glove box
or a butterfly on a bell,
you can't park here.

More Tales from the Crypt

Despite its supposed jeweled movement
and rocket mechanics, my new heart's
no more accurate, bowstring
still snapped, kitten just as frazzled.
They wouldn't let me keep my old heart
because it was sliced out and burned
so I wasn't able to take a bite
like any warrior would his enemy's
to become a greater warrior. Nope.
Apparently not even worth dissecting
or feeding to that starved lion
rescued from a Dallas junkyard,
never to be jarred in my office
between my alien skull and complete
works of Vesalius and Sun Ra
to show where poetry comes from
like when Matthew smashed through
a plate-glass door and just kept going.

Paul's Window

Watching a storm crab-walk
on lightning stilts
out of Manhattan, and a physics book
I'm reading says gravity
isn't a force, it's more a ripple,
pucker, a funnel in space
a falling thing is a marble in
rolling round and down.
Hanging on Paul's wall—
an upside-down guy falls through
streaky black stuff same as he's made of,
his expression too coarsely rendered
to make out any panic or relief
which seems partly the artist's
intention. It's night.
Like that makes any difference.

IV Drip

Where it rains, my hand hurts.
A root laces the lighthouse.
Water splashed on my face before
I have a face becomes my face.
I'm trying to avoid the distinct
impressions of inhabiting a different
dimension. Sometimes sexually,
sometimes in a letter. I remember,
not with enough certainty to be sure
he wasn't me, some loon on the 6th floor
raving he just needs to see a beach again,
starfish and giant ear-shaped rock,
silver horizon blasted apart.

End of Life Ode

I was taught even a turtle
could be your emissary. You
introduced yourself with a yellow
ghost-hand coming from the radiator
which no one believed me about,
a rusty nail in the backyard
which was empirical enough,
pneumonia more so but it's not
until 50 years later on the table,
you're floating in still, black water,
slightly brackish, slightly lilac.
Light? None. Nor any tonk of boat
tugged along, no royal roar of familiar
meow. Not a single candle or gavel
then I come to strapped to a sundial
of you, the names of immunosuppressants
like those of archangels. Slowly I untubed
like a cricket from gluely cobwebs
although I'm never far from you was I
ever? Even this muffin can bring me
to tears knowing you're almost here,
most designated driver among the blossoms
falling into my vodka. Darling, open
your kimono for me.

The Institutionalization of American Poetry

1. I Too Fucking Hate It

Once we realized all the commotion
was caused by insect wings,
we could all feel more helpless
which provides empowerment
to those who shouldn't have it:
millionaires, department chairs, hood ornaments,
everyone so afraid of counterattack,
the only safe statue is faceless,
the moon's demonized
but there's sure plenty of mascara.
The long view fills with smoke,
maybe a tree if there's any imagination left,
more likely a pile of hashtags and complaints
and a long exposé of the digestive systems
of worms.

2. The Poet-Scholar

My studies in human potential
collapsed when I joined an English department.
It's not as funny as you'd think
watching lobsters try to masturbate
then scuttle forth to form mutual-admiration
tribunals. Sometimes a balloon floats over
like a clown's suicide note. Sometimes
if the wind's right, the sky low,
I can hear the sea's I-told-you-so.
End of poem.

3. Clown Suicide Note

Became the Nowhere Chair of Poetry
after years of internment
in previous mental facilities.
Published 15 volumes of verse from which
a few tentacles may have emerged.
Married twice and got a heart transplant
apparently to increase pain tolerance.
There's a reason warthogs aren't farmed
but no way can anyone say Dean Young
lived a life of smaller and smaller mistakes.
Beep beep. Uh huh. Yup,
it'll take a few more balloons
to get this thing aloft.
A squirting boutonniere,
a mood of quiet ejecta.
David and Dobby get my books.
Joe, don't let anyone see this—
I'd hate for my last readers to be cops.
Indeed that's my head singing in the bricks
as some feral cats finish off the softer parts.
I bet that drawing Tomaž wrote on
is worth something now.
Samantha, disperse the dragons!

Pep Talk in a Crater

Even though your engine light's blinking,
your bicycle's been stolen and your heart's
a mangle, try not to listen to the crow's
opinion no matter your concurrence,
no matter the frog's disquisition in its frog jar
or the shalt-nots of dawn.
Often I too have been chased barefoot
by I know not what. Often a meadow
struggles to mention itself. Thus
someone can start out a column of flames
and be moth-dust by afternoon.
Thus another can collapse in on herself
like a neutron star. All we know for sure
is Mozart took a lot of hammering
and all those trees had to be screwed in.
Once the little green wings are smashed
from the wedding vessels, it's ok
to feel like you're watching your own murder
with a butterscotch in your mouth,
like how laughing makes the coffin
easier to carry, the usual rueful decorums
masking the want-my-mommy,
this-ain't-my-planet wail.
Dumpster in the front yard yellow.
Knock-knock joke in ICU.
No one knows who's there
so keep guessing. How about
a burning scarecrow seeking blood donations?
Another reverend of alienation soliciting

for the latest political roller derby?
Spaceman on a snapped cord?
Lost dog and his kittens?
Go ahead, invite the Witnesses in
to poke fun at their weeny leviathan.
You call that an apocalypse?
While we may assume no immediate danger,
it can't hurt but to avail yourself of the hatchet
in the hatchery and a good red.
Obviously god needs lots of purple
streaks in his design.

Corpse Pose

It's not like there's a sound,
no caterwaul or oceanic gasp,
no popping root hairs of a carrot
yanked but I'm looking down
on my body growing translucent,
a single set of clown teeth
chattering inside. Huh.
So I guess I have a soul after all,
it wasn't just my hamster's death
causing a lump or that electric snap
when I first saw Niki, neither
1,000 doves impaling themselves
on a glass dagger as Breton said it was
nor some palooka's boxing glove.
I shouldn't have expected so much
from sex, 3-D printers, and swans
but it wasn't that awful stalled
in the blizzard. Of course the lecture
goes on forever but it's almost funny,
falling from the vascular tree.
Tiny spiders live so high
they must survive on air.
My body hates my soul, how
it stays so skinny thriving on air,
never hungover, never hit with fist
or restraining order, defying
that old dualism, flirting at the party
like it's never been spurned.

Ant-Head Sutures

Once when I was in trouble,
I got my aura photographed.
Green grapefruit with a purple

dogleg where my heart should be.
Perhaps devoured by a wound.
Perhaps stuck in an orchid's throat.

Maybe moths on a birthday cake,
glitter in orbit. I can't answer
for the stars but they seem sheepish

in their brilliance, shaking
on their daffodil stalks.
Once I too fell over 30 feet

eventually caught by a thicker limb,
that's how good life can be,
and I haven't even mentioned the taste

of snow on a beach or my darling
bent over a hotel bed or how
it's just a single protein missing

that stops us from bioluminescing
and there's no such thing as death,
just darkness
and darkness never hurt anyone.

Milkweed

Bright things rise in ripples
like asterisks on fire.
It's ok to toss a skull around.
We are all toys of something.
I myself am a top.
Almost autumn,
this green disguise is getting crinkly.
Even at 60,
we all have to go back to school.
Smell of sharpened pencils—
does anyone know what that is anymore?
Is there anyone out there?

Daily Apocalypse

Saw a door on a truck going by
swing open.
Saw a guy in an acid-yellow
vest inspecting the corner
green puddle that never evaporates
wave as if waving me in.
A mockingbird concurred
with a car alarm. Someone
had dropped a purple spaceman in.
Aphrodite rose from the mist
as crazily as flowers eat meat.
Tried to go to a museum
but ended up in a weapons depot,
everyone stunned like there's a hole
in their chest and they're struggling
through peacock guts. Is Beatlemania
at last dead? How about English departments?
The soul we know is iron. Plunged from fire
into ice, it shines. One of these days,
I'll refuse to fill out the green form
just to get the blue form as if
everything isn't already permanently
seething formlessness and meat-eating flowers.
I'm just like you.
I wasn't made by their god.
My vote never counts.

8,000 Whispers

Befriend a ricochet.

Overshadow the funeral.

Hunger is strength.

Hunger is tranquillity.

Crush thyme.

Eat her body.

Translucent heart.

Spinal fire spiral.

What strange wolves

we've welcomed to our waltz.

Sub Club Punch Card

Another morning of my body lifting me
like a lion its prey, like an osprey,

not nearly as fixated on death
as my dreams might make you think

if ants streaming from an alarm clock
are any indication, ditto black moths

hatching from the closet of my chest
like bits of glass from a harpsichord.

I'm only 45% black moths to Lorca's 80
but at least we're both 90% water.

Like carrots. Genetically, I'm a dirty
lake. My blood type is Sauvignon. O

body and its fucking gushes, gashes,
jury duty and hot flashes, appendages

perfect for falling from trees, a temporary
lease above a tanning booth, data far

from any proof, a home security system,
long-forgotten code.

Parthenogenesis

There is nothing wrong
with your stem. The goat
eats god. Good for the goat,
good for god, especially
good for the cheese.
No need to give night
more agency than it already has.
There is nothing wrong
with your radio, the trumpet
just refuses to sleep.
Stand in the doorway
until you hear the all clear.
It's snowing on the Parthenon.

Genesis Pants

In the beginning there was nothing
but a lot of blinking
and the sense of being unable to sleep
like in a French movie.
Ok, maybe some heavy breathing.
Can't be helped.
But there were no defibrillators in terminals,
no tiny suicidal chessmen sucked up by the vacuum,
no honey-baked ham
although there was a space for it,
a huge kinda creepy ham-shaped conceptual space
which hurt
which is why some mistaken tribes
worship a god-headache
and all there is is politics
when anyone with two antennae knows
all there is is a turtle
in a deep dark pool
like the idea of an oak in an acorn
or intercourse in a nun.
Finally—who wouldn't?—the turtle
gets bored sick and pukes
and according to Tomaž who was there
the puke turned to quartz
which as we know constitutes
30% of Earth's crust
and is basically electricity personified
so for the next 800 years
while trying to walk upright,

the people search for extension cords,
Descartes saying they're all in the mind,
Bacon saying for god's sake, look around
so the people start using words like
lacunae, flying buttress, Quetzalcoatl, Ragnarok,
reification immunosuppressant autospell
to justify their behavior,
how they burst into tears at sunset
then try to shoot it.
Who knows where all these people come from
although clay and hyena grease seem likely.
Something dense, nonconductive that picks up lint
and won't bounce.
Something under-the-wading-pool icky
starting arguments with lizards and rivers,
amoebas and themselves until a huge hand
comes out of the clouds clutching a beating
heart which is no help because
as Tomaž tells it after a couple of good belts,
only he sees it.

My Life as a Hatchet

Beware, my friends, of the misarticulated
mannequins that stalk these halls because
once they think you're one of their own,
they'll criticize your walk, how

you won't march or take your sunglasses off
during the committee meeting, how
unabashed you are at their end-
of-the-world edicts, how inappropriate

your laugh, sword cane, flaming-skull
shot glass. An orange potato trolls
the White House. If you didn't wake up
screaming, you didn't wake up.

Refinery Fire

Maybe no one believes anything I say
because my ears are so small, my face
looks like another face is under it
which even I admit, peeping through
its ports, seems shifty like the only
sober guy at the crash site, like singing
at the funeral while keeping a blizzard
on life support, neutrinos constantly
hurtling through us bright bits
through bright emptiness so no wonder
the mirror's tired of being a mirror
and wants to be water again, dark water
and the horse wants to be a proscenium arch
and the flower wants teeth and you
can stand in your own kitchen
and still be miles from yourself.
No wonder most of our thoughts never reach
themselves, lacunae in our chrysocolla,
mulberry trees hardly clinging to the earth.
Goddamn twig magnificent. Goddamn worm.
A ship sets off. It's very cold.
The snow takes its face from a moth.

Early Study in Levitation

Piranha that's always with me
gnawing at the lockbox is almost
proof enough that life might be
worth living. Ditto that berserk dog
in berserker forsythia behind
the burned church on 4th making friendly
and that moment when Ben Webster
just breathes through his horn
Ira and I talked over while his bunny
ate my shoelace. Some people just let
their bunnies run wild, some study
clouds, some spend all day in the graveyard
falling in love. They're the scientists
of spring and we can't do without them.
All musicians are metaphysicians
but poets... even Sylvia Plath
had to eat a lot of dirt
to get to the azurite, even
Wordsworth needed a dog.
Welcome, lacunae!
Brighten, mind!
Welcome, spine turned iridescent flight-dust,
disproportionate emotional response
to wolves and violets.
What Mary said.
A green pill.
A tree.
A prokaryotic fidelity to the sea.

A Rhythmia

A mallet stops a horse race.
There is a dwarf in my face.
I rewind emptiness.
It rains in my raincoat.
A glance of glitter dislodges
every cornea.

Among Bulrushes and Sky Scrapers

I don't know if Tomaž
was scattered into the Hippocrene
or baked into a heavy, seedy peasant bread
to break among his young acolytes
like wedding cake but everyone says
his death mask smiles. No surprise,
even the chameleon on the window
trying to turn translucent smiles.
Ditto redwing feather. A green
puddle of antifreeze that never
evaporates, a forest fire smiles
the same as a mollusk, so too
Tiepolo's pink monsters. Your hand
will smile inside a wave like water
smiles after swallowed like a candle
during a power outage. The skull
permanently smiles so what
are we worried about?

Wheelbarrow with Wings

The trouble with teaching poetry is
everyone already knows what it is.
Some insects are born pregnant, others launch
themselves on filaments of silk so try
coming up with a grading policy for that.
The best thing is cramming as many mulberries
into the mechanism as possible.
It's just like on the moon, same
bulbous heads, same lack of gravity
so you can propel yourself into orbit
with a good sneeze. The design
of the martini glass—is it to emphasize
our tipsiness or provide sufficient reflecting
surface so we can see we're sipping sky?
Trick question. Either/or is a false
dichotomy. Extra credit if you answered
all the above. If you can't swim,
dancing furiously in the deep end
will keep you afloat.

My Process

Sometimes it's like pushing a wheelchair
of bones through high-tide sand.
Like giving birth to an ostrich,
an ostrich with antlers that glow.
The sense there's something wrong and
not giving a hoot like going to church
to see what you can steal. Experimental
turn signal, neurotransmitter's whim.
Mythologically, by the time Orpheus
gets the message, it's obscured
by radiance having been delivered
by a trickster god. Of course,
the operatic head floats down the river,
decapitation making for a better singer
as with a praying mantis. Zigzag
in a plaid forest, it's like lying
fully clothed under motel covers.
Lavender spit, amniotic gin.
It's like trying to be a cube of light
undissolved in a bigger cube of light,
like holding your own brain and
wringing it out. The heart has nothing
to do with it. The heart has everything
to do with it, floating like a jellyfish
all bioluminescent sting, monkeys
ripping the car chrome off
while we tour the ruins.

Unprotected

It's been days since hoppy frog was wound up
but he's still got jump.
Like a dead bee.
Like a liberal arts education.
Like a tree storing lightning inside itself.
Like a window broken in a good way.
Like cardiac tissue.
Like when the apprentice assigned
to paint the background shrubbery
has some sort of seizure
like when the soul blazes out in the eternal
and pierces your foot
like in Blake.
Not torn in two with gray claws.
Not rotting deep in the pancreas.
Not being hung upside down.
Not the stabbed-out eye of a peacock.
Not losing your virginity to a scarecrow.
The sky will fill our graves.
The sea is entirely bells.
I love you.

Sleepers Awake

I don't want to start the day
with a list of what makes me sad
so I cancel that appointment,
put away the X-rays, put on my torn
red shirt and hug my darling
hard enough to taste the beach
on her shoulder. How's she do that
1,000 miles from the sea? Unfurtively,
I admire her breasts which isn't creepy
because of our relationship during which
time spent washing dishes, changing
air filters and picking up dog poop, etc.
must be equal to or less than
the time spent admiring her breasts
from my perspective. In fact, the whole
waterproof getup of that body she's wearing
which fits perfectly without scrunching
or pinching. I like how she can sit down
and stand up and hop without ripping.
I lick the places where it attaches to her soul.
They taste like alfalfa.

Little Back-Row DY

Falling apart never sounded bad.
You fell apart and stayed in your room
painting the hair of your Bride
of Frankenstein model green.
No one expected you to do a report on Peru.
Once I smashed an alarm clock with a shoe
carefully. What happened was like a cow
taken apart and eaten
only without blood.
I didn't swallow any of it,
just put one geary thing in my mouth.
Once I licked a gun, it tasted the same.
My mom cried and yelled a lot.
My father worked at night.
I thought it would be lucky
never having to go to sleep
except when it made you want to kill everyone.
There was something wrong with the vacuum.
If you touched the scaly boy at school
that was it.
I had trouble enunciating
because of my malocclusion.
That's how I learned a lot of words.
A plethora of words.
To substitute.
Most words were in my head.
I liked how *word* was almost *world*.
Words always lead to other words
unless you're talking to a girl you like.

If you tell her about her nimbus,
she'll laugh at you with her friends.
Can't be helped.
The authority of Santa Claus
was deeply undermined by the Easter Bunny
and don't even get me started on the tooth fairy.
One day the president was shot.
We got out of social studies.
I never went home without first
checking the UFO crash site in the woods.
Some of the ground was turned to glass.
Once during a funeral for a cardinal
I heard god climbing around in the pine limbs.
He was awkward.
I was good at science my teacher said
because I got excited about grasshoppers
having ears in their legs.
Auditory receptors.
Sometimes I'd try to sneak
extra esses in *grasshopper.*
Grassssshoppersssss.
I drew an eye on the back of my right hand
but the other one didn't turn out
because that hand writes messy.
Once I saw my teacher at the store.
She had a watermelon in her cart
rolling around like a green head.
It was funny and I hid.
Why don't people make jack-o'-lanterns
out of watermelons?
It's already red inside.

I started out as a speck.
So did the universe.
Only half the weight of everything
is rational.
One of my sisters was in an asylum.
No one used the word *asylum*.
I'd say it slower even
than my enunciation lessons
so nothing would come out.
Asylum.
She was getting therapy
for nerves that ran in the family.
My favorite thing about chalk is the dust.
Ants can stay a long time underwater.
They carry down a bubble.

To Poetry

The first you I tried to write
had a penguin and made me happy
to be with you even if, actually
because I couldn't understand you,
not what your atomic number was or why
O why you're so flocked with the creepy
and the dull when you can blow up the world
then origami it into a cosmic rose.
Half the time you're tilling through
my solar plexus, half I can't find you
anywhere and half you're Shari
letting me hold her canary
for cleansing. No, you don't add up
although you make some crazy square
roots and repeating decimals. Composed
of conspiracies of vowels, voices, voices,
a huge rectangle full of sticky notes,
glory in a leaf, the aster in disaster,
and—why not?—a new bill of rights.
Something reaches out of you
with a red trophy to whoever
approacheth you nude but
the Texas legislature hates you,
wants you out of college curricula
like Thomas Jefferson and evolution
out of textbooks. You, of course,
are above it all like a let-go kite
as well as below vascularizing crypts.
Maybe there ain't no such thing as death,

just shucked worm casts. Moondust
tastes like gunpowder and the universe,
we're told, is beige, a color known
to absorb pain. Poetry, I love
you certainly without any irritable
reaching after fact. Resistance
makes you shine.

Big Fun

First gladioli.
Gladioli with synaptic urge.
Bigger and bigger chirps.
Then squid. Wet gloves.
A bank statement origami'd into a dove.
Ignoring the protocol at the cyclotron.
Rust dissolving into something warm.
Grasshopper in a bell.
Helping an injured limb out of the road.
Fragility central to the process.
Like no one knows where this bolt's fallen from.
Like putting something in a bag too small
and ending on a preposition.
Like the head has a balcony
to throw itself from.
Lightning-struck quartz sings.
Like jumping into petals.
Darkness soft and without rind.
Light that hurts a lot less
once you realize which parts
of yourself are burning,
which for show.
Suffering is just a ticket stub
and divorce a spree.
Then, eventually, eagles.

Red Hots on a Cupcake

When having sex, I much prefer
someone else having sex
on the other end. Or the same end.
Or without end. Just lots of lost pets
come home, foam, receptive moans
cresting with each thrust like the world's
most gorgeous dog-toy. More people
have sex in Chevrolets than during
Star Trek recent findings suggest
which I can't understand. Ditto nearly
anything in Latin except cunnilingus
which means the ocean is a tongue
and who doesn't want to come while
someone from the future says, Beam me up?
Not that teleportation wouldn't be redundant.
Should our eyes open and meet: much
pandemonium among the angels
in the armory as promised. What
I love about experts is get enough
together to study whatever rosebush,
paramecium, orgasm, reason itself,
half conclude it doesn't exist as if
you didn't just prick yourself on a cloud.
Just because something doesn't exist
doesn't mean it's not dropping petals
into your vodka right now. Everything gets
greener, a wing comes out of the mouth.
Under every river is another river
and under that, an aerie.

My Collage Life

So after being chopped apart,
sewn back together from mostly
the same stuff, some 70s prog rock
still sticking out, some Kafka fluff,
how's it feel to still be alive where you are?
Like a bee in a bubble bath.
A cigarette in a French movie.
The single golden scrawl
in one of Paul's black paintings.
A piece of sky upside down
possibly from a different puzzle entirely.
Like that turtle we stopped traffic for.
Sometimes a cloud intervenes.
Periods of asterisks.
No one knows what they are either.
Like simultaneously being a part
of something big and very very small.
Trismegistus in an azurite crown.
Two carbon atoms per cubic meter of outer space.
A glove that tugs itself off
always ends up inside out.
Like digging a trench, filling it with blood,
waiting for consultation.
First one out of the horse and hacking.
Like a winged presence in the wings
beckoning stage left.
The heft of cathedral tunes.
Exit pursued.
Cog in a crocodile.

Codicil in an organelle.
Another coil in the outer shell.
Like squeezing lemons lets you know
just how cut up your hands are.
When Debussy in the afterlife
heard about the atomic bomb,
he needed to be alone with his gazelles.
Like through the hole in my chest
comes the conveyance.
Like being turned into a swan.
Being in complete agreement with the moon
and anything that survives exclusively
on nectar. Laughter too, just not yet
close enough to tell about what.

The Demystification Process

They take ping-pong out of the break room.
The boys in R&D coming up with more
and more outré transparencies until
a whole generation can't tell the difference
between an anal exam and poetry,
the lepton still in a fog.
Initially, the plan may have been conceived in a dream
but subsequent iterations
obviously threw the throb way off.
It's a short dependent clause but
by its end, Mrs. Ramsay's gone. For 15 minutes,
someone was declared a genius
for spraying everything black
but that just created a new kind of sticky.
Indeed, it may be the collapse
of the hierophantic excesses of modernism
that completes the dissolution of volumetric form
but that doesn't stop us shattering
against that huge concave piece of plexiglass
barring the cosmos. The stinger goes through
the eye, hits the back of the throat
then ricochets all over. Kiss me, elevator.
Kiss me, amorphous shape at the end of the dock.
3,000 sexual harassment compliance videos later,
people are still on their knees in restrooms
weeping with flowers in their hair.

Small Craft Talk Warning

All poetry is a form of hope.
A duck walks into a bar.
An abandoned space station crashes to earth.
When probing the monster's brain,
you're probably probing your own.
A beautiful woman turns into a ghost.
I hope never to miscalculate the dosage
that led to the infarction
of my laboratory rabbit again.
All poetry is a form of hope.
Not certain, just actual
like love and other traffic circles.
I cried on that airplane too,
Midwest patchwork below
like a board game on which mythic
forces kick apart the avatars.
I always want to be the race car,
usually end up a thumbtack.
When I was young, sitting in a tree
counted as preparation and later
maybe a little whoopee in the morgue.
So go ahead, thaw the alien, break
the pentagram but watch out for
the hordes of institutional fops.
It's not a museum, it's a hive.
The blood may be fake
but the bleeding's not.

Fade Out

The flashlight my sister swept
across the heavens got no response
either. When my friend leaves his lab,
he still limps and our government's demanding
funerals for aborted fetuses and where's
a fetus gonna get the dough for that?
Today I found a chunk of quartz
with a face inside you could tell
was willing to wait another million years
for its scream to reach the surface
let that be a lesson. Ditto when the same
cuckoo that followed Tomaž from China
tries to follow me but gets slapped back
for groping the moon, don't I just?
Maybe Jay's right that it all comes down
to one untranslatable fragment from Parmenides.
Like when a child is covered with petals
or a goat receives a necklace of bells.
It's just a thin thread that holds
the body to the soul. Visibility
is a disguise.

The Science of Thunder

One day while I was alive
in my pajamas, not yet threatened
my love would leave me
to sort out my rebuffed retirement alone
and erase myself with lemon haze
and my knife skills were still developing
and I could get to the river
in 20 minutes solely through alleys
befriending sad, wacko dogs with a few biscuits
and a huge green spider rappelling toward me
like the long-lost eye of my idol
and Jim was alive and sent honey
with stingers in it and Tomaž
was alive and sent postcards from Bled
which looks idyllically exsanguinated
and no one yet had told me my little tail
was monstrous or drawing a house
upside down on blue horns of ice
with an eyeball inside was wrong
and that sugar and salt will kill you
and if that's a mouse in the kitchen
and if you dream you're falling
and you can't look at the corona
and lightning bugs are cannibals,
all the warm electric bodies
racked with pain because god
is insane and made of velvet thorns
and you can't swim alone,
I thought I could distinguish sunshine

from the flames of hell and withstand
the fucked-up beauty of this world
and not that I'm sure there is one the next.

Silly String

A seat is being prepared for us
in the rain.
A lily has been prepared.
The catalogue of loss comes to an end
regardless of the punctuation.
If you stopped reading at page 45,
Gatsby never dies,
the rules that govern this whole operatic shtick
written down and erased so many times,
who's surprised a marriage turns into
mush, a vow just idiot sound?
Pretty much doesn't mean a thing
like most hymns.
And for those of us looking ahead,
there interposes an ambulance.
Someone's washing chrysanthemums
in the parking lot. Someone's hefting
body-size bags of dog food into a truck.
The kaleidoscope remains the most
efficacious diagnostic instrument
for those of us who've been shattered.
There's so much I can't explain
if someone would just give me the chance.

Acknowledgments

Thanks to the editors of the following publications where some of the poems in this book have appeared: *The American Poetry Review; Conduit; Forklift, Ohio; jubilat; The Massachusetts Review; Ploughshares; Poetry;* and *The Threepenny Review.*

A few of these poems were used in the musical project *Good Day for Cloud Fishing* with Ben Goldberg, Ron Miles, and Nels Cline.

Gratitude to Dobby Gibson, Kevin Stein, Matt Hart, Joe Di Prisco, David Schaefer, Skyler Osborne, Nick Miller, Claire Bowen, David Breskin, and Samantha Karas who boosted the process. And to the perpetually Shifting Foundation, thank you.

About the Author

Dean Young was born in Columbia, Pennsylvania, and received his MFA from Indiana University. His collections of poetry include *Strike Anywhere* (1995), winner of the Colorado Prize for Poetry; *Skid* (2002), finalist for the Lenore Marshall Poetry Prize; *elegy on toy piano* (2005), finalist for the Pulitzer Prize; *Primitive Mentor* (2008), shortlisted for the International Griffin Poetry Prize; *Bender: New & Selected Poems* (2012); and *Shock by Shock* (2015). He has also written a book on poetics, *The Art of Recklessness: Poetry as Assertive Force and Contradiction* (2010).

Poetry is vital to language and living. Since 1972, Copper Canyon Press has published extraordinary poetry from around the world to engage the imaginations and intellects of readers, writers, booksellers, librarians, teachers, students, and donors.

WE ARE GRATEFUL FOR THE MAJOR SUPPORT PROVIDED BY:

THE PAUL G. ALLEN
FAMILY FOUNDATION

TO LEARN MORE ABOUT UNDERWRITING
COPPER CANYON PRESS TITLES,
PLEASE CALL 360-385-4925 EXT. 103

WE ARE GRATEFUL FOR THE MAJOR SUPPORT PROVIDED BY:

Anonymous

Jill Baker and Jeffrey Bishop

Anne and Geoffrey Barker

Donna and Matt Bellew

John Branch

Diana Broze

The Beatrice R. and Joseph A.
  Coleman Foundation Inc.

The Currie Family Fund

Laurie and Oskar Eustis

Mimi Gardner Gates

Nancy Gifford

Gull Industries Inc. on behalf of
  William True

The Trust of Warren A. Gummow

Carolyn and Robert Hedin

Bruce Kahn

Phil Kovacevich and Eric Wechsler

Lakeside Industries Inc. on behalf
  of Jeanne Marie Lee

Maureen Lee and Mark Busto

Peter Lewis

Ellie Mathews and Carl Youngmann
  as The North Press

Hank Meijer

Gregg Orr

Petunia Charitable Fund and
  adviser Elizabeth Hebert

Gay Phinny

Suzie Rapp and Mark Hamilton

Emily and Dan Raymond

Jill and Bill Ruckelshaus

Cynthia Sears

Kim and Jeff Seely

Richard Swank

Dan Waggoner

Barbara and Charles Wright

Caleb Young as C. Young Creative

The dedicated interns and
  faithful volunteers of
  Copper Canyon Press

The Chinese character for poetry is made up of two parts:
"word" and "temple." It also serves as pressmark for
Copper Canyon Press.

The poems are set in Fournier.
Book design and composition by Phil Kovacevich.